GET UP...AND LIVE

Roshunda D. Atchison

Get Up...And Live by Roshunda D. Atchison
ISBN #: 13: 978-0692872000
　　　　　10: 0692872000

Copyright ©2017 by Roshunda D. Atchison

Scripture quotations are taken from the HOLY BIBLE, COMMON ENGLISH VERSION, Copyright © 2011. Used by permission. All rights reserved.

Published by:
Judah House Publishing
6838 Lost Thicket
Houston, Texas 77085

Printed in the United States of America
All rights reserved. Under International Copyright Law, no part of this publication may be reproduced, stored, or transmitted by any means without written permission from the Publisher.

This book is dedicated to every person who had the faith to experience outside-the-cage living. To every person who held his or her breath afraid of what the next breath might bring. To every person who dared to hold on to his or her dreams when life tried to snatch them away. To every person who loved with a broken heart, embraced despite fear, and continued to walk even in the darkness where doubt and anxiety dwelled. To the survivors who made people believe in the power of hope.

This book is dedicated to those who are unique and peculiar, who dance to the beat of their own drum. This book is dedicated to…

LOVE.

CONTENTS

Preface..5

Part I: Get Up…...............................7
   Chapter 1
   How Did I Get Here? I'm Not Supposed to
   Be Here!...8
   Chapter 2
   Why Did I Stay Here?........................16
   Chapter 3
   Get Up or Shut Up!............................25

Part II: …And Live........................33
   Chapter 4
   …Without Paralyzing Fear...................34
   Chapter 5
   …Without Pain....................................41
   Chapter 6
   …In Peace...45
   Chapter 7
   …Like It's Golden..............................49

Final Thought..................................53

PREFACE

This book was birthed with so many tears. I can give so many reasons for writing this book, but this book exists simply because my heart desired freedom.

This journey has been difficult yet beautiful at the same time. I remember many nights when I sat at my writing desk, listening to instrumental worship music. The music soothed my pain as I dug deep to pull out the hurt and damaged pieces of myself, to lay them out on display for the entire world to see. For me, each written word was a liberating tear. The journey was beautiful. What started as a silent scream for help evolved into a piece of my legacy that I hope will not only motivate and inspire but will transform lives.

If you have ever questioned your worthiness, felt invisible, or questioned your life's meaning, this is the perfect book for you. My hope is that this book will help you discover the greatness that lives inside of you and that is pushing to come out. My hope is that this book ignites something in you that you thought was long dead. Make your journey marvelous, and I'll see you on the other side.

PART I
GET UP...

When life knocks you down, try to land on your back. Because if you can look up, you can get up. Let your reason get you back up.
—Les Brown

The greatest glory in living lies not in never falling, but in rising every time we fall.
—Nelson Mandela

When life knocks you down, get back up and fight harder.
—Unknown

CHAPTER 1

HOW DID I GET HERE? I'M NOT SUPPOSED TO BE HERE!

As I lay in my bed, I clearly heard in my spirit, "Get up and live." I jumped up and prepared for my day, but there was something different about this particular morning. I felt a great urgency within me, a new excitement about facing this day and every day thereafter. I pondered this directive all day. I call it a "directive" because I believe that it was an authoritative instruction from God. The charge not only shifted my mind but my spirit and my emotions. The energy that I was feeling was not reflective of the emotional prior weeks' energy. I went from being unable to control my emotions—from being angry one moment to crying the next—to feeling like a person who was seeing the world for the first time. My entire life, I have heard slogans, quotes, and sayings that were meant to encourage: "Pull yourself up by the bootstraps," "Pull your pants up, tighten your belt, and keep going," and, my favorite, "Dust yourself off, and keep moving." All of these sayings can be helpful at times, but when the issues of life come to a head, that's all that they are: slogans, quotes, and sayings, with no real power to impact the hearer.

How did I get *Here?* Prior to this day, I had asked myself this question many times. As young children, we dream big, but as life happens, it whittles away at that big dream. The dream morphs into something that is unrecognizable to the dreamer, and sometimes it lands in the desert of nonexistence. One day you look at your life, consider your defeats, and ask yourself, "How did I get *Here?*"

What is *Here?* Here is a place where sadness reigns, where low self-esteem is the norm, and where rejection is the gatekeeper—a place of defeat. Here is the incubator of dying dreams. Hope is on life support in this place called Here. You can reside Here so long that you are unable to determine when you took up residence.

A person does not enter this world with a belief that he or she will not achieve anything or will not be the best expression of himself or herself. We are not born into this world hopeless and without dreams. Before we take our first breath on this earth, we already have dreams and purpose inside us, waiting to be discovered and lived out. We come to this world with gifts and vision to bless the world and make it a better place because we lived in it.

It may take time for some of us to discover this vision, but it is already inside of us. Every earthen vessel has hidden treasure inside. It is our responsibility and lifelong goal to reveal that treasure to the world, to make a deposit. It is not in God's plan that we live in this place called Here that I've just described: a place of despair, of hopelessness, of sorrow, of sadness, of rejections, a place where everything that can stop us from walking in our purpose and fulfilling why we are on this earth originates and resides. The answer to the daunting question "Why am I Here?" lingers on; however, with certainty I can clearly state that I'm not supposed to be Here.

Perhaps my entry to Here was because I was rejected at birth. For a great part of my life, I have felt rejected and like I did not fit in. Rejection has a way of making you feel like you are never good enough. So, you spend your life trying to prove that you are worthy of a little love and that you are enough. You live your life silently screaming, "Look at me!" You are always performing, always begging for just a hint of love and acceptance.

My mother would always tell me the story of how my father rejected me before I was born. He did not acknowledge that I was his child until I was born and resembled him. He is no longer with us in this existence of life, but I was like his twin, and he loved me as he knew how to love. Every time my mother told the story, it cut deep within my heart. Each cut chipped away at my feeling of worthiness. I wondered why my mother told the story so many times. Now, I understand that she was also an object of rejection, in a different way. Who knows how much time it took and the strength that she had to muster up to even speak about it. Maybe talking about the situation was her way of dealing with the pain of the rejection. Maybe it was her way of releasing the hurt and of getting the freedom that she so needed.

Perhaps my entry to Here was because of the silence. Growing up in a silent household and family hinders your ability to express yourself. In my home, we just did not mention certain things, ask certain questions, or say certain things. *Silence.* Trust me, I love my parents very much, and this is not a fault-finding trip, because I know that they did the best that they knew and were taught to do. Likewise, I am certain my daughter has her list of complaints about me. However, liberation requires truth. It was not until I studied my parents' genealogy that I truly came to understand why they were the way they were. Now I understand that they were familiar with this place called Here. I understand that they had unrealized dreams, quenched desires in life, and missed opportunities to reveal the treasures that God placed in them.

The words "I love you" were foreign in our household. My parents took care of us because they loved us, but they rarely expressed their love verbally.

Expression is powerful. Sometimes your ears want to hear what your heart knows. I remember being afraid to express myself, to talk about life issues, to ask questions. So, I remained silent. I took that silence into my adult life. I was afraid to express my truth.

I was living in a loud world, but I had no voice because I did not know how to express my inner feelings. Expression is powerful because life and death are in the power of the tongue. When God expressed/spoke, things came into existence. Expression fills voids in the spirit. Expression strengthens the heart. Expression builds relationships and opens doors to understanding.

Perhaps my entry to Here was because of the life choices that I made. A stream of failed relationships will get you to Here. A marriage where love is questionable will get you to Here. An unsuccessful career will get you to Here. An ineffective ministry will get you to Here. Unrealized dreams and unnecessary sacrifices will get you to Here. Unmanaged money and bankruptcy will get you to Here. A series of failures and disappointments will cause you to settle for Here. We all have made choices in our lives that we wish we could go back in time and rethink.

Liberation begins with the revelation that in all situations we have a choice. There are several factors that are beyond our control, but we still have the choice how we response to those factors.

We all have our reasons why we are in a place that we were never meant to occupy. Some have visited, and some reside, but we can all escape this place called Here. We can all get up and live—live our best life. Acknowledging and taking responsibility for our own choices is a power step toward liberation. Most of the time we are holding the gun to our own heads when we make these type of life choices. Forgiving yourself, healing, and moving forward is the key. I am a firm believer that everything works for our good. With every choice, there are consequences, good and bad.

Whichever way my choice work out, there is a lesson to be learned with every experience: A lesson that has the power to make me better. A lesson of healing. A lesson that results in more faith.

We are not our failed choices, nor are we bad because of bad decisions. These are events that happen while living, a series of events called life. We can choose to allow the experiences to help us soar or keep us grounded in the unproductive place called Here.

Do you hear it yet? Can you feel it yet? The sound in your ears and tug on your heart so that you might get up and live.

CHAPTER 2

WHY DID I STAY HERE?

"Why?" is always a good question, but it is the answer to the question that is problematic. There is always an answer, whether we are willing to admit it. Why do you choose to stay in a situation that you know is not healthy? Why do you stand still when you know that some type of action is required? Why do you continue to travel down an unproductive road? Why do you stay in a place, as I described in Chapter 1, where sadness reigns, low self-esteem is the norm, and rejection is the gatekeeper?

I believe that at the root of every questionable and contrary decision is fear. Fear will tell you that you are not worthy of any type of love or happiness. Fear will convince you that you are not enough. Fear will trick you into believing that your life does not matter and that life is safer in your little comfort zone. So, you accept everything that fear has told you as your truth, and you wander aimlessly through life, just existing—continually in a state of denial and refusing to face that you are destined to live, and not just live, but live an abundant life.

God never envisioned for man to be held captive to fear. It was never His plan for man to operate as if fear was a part of mankind's DNA. Jesus died so that we would not have to be tormented by fear and the fruit of fear. But when we open the door to fear, it becomes engrafted into our DNA. Even though God's word repeatedly admonishes us not to fear, but only to believe, we continue to allow ourselves to become slaves to fear. We fear and we stay in this place called Here.

Fear is an unpleasant emotion usually caused by a perceived threat of harm or pain. Fear, whether real or imagined, can paralyze us and prevent progress. It is the main reason why the physical graveyard is so rich with books that were not written, businesses that were never formed, opportunities that were missed, and dreams that were never realized or brought to fruition. Sadly, the people were buried with the dreams, gifts, and visions that were meant to be released into this world.

At one point in my life, I found myself in a vicious cycle of fear. Fear of failure stopped me from executing my ideas, and because I did not execute them, I feared that I would fail. As the cycle continued, because I feared that I would fail, I did not execute my ideas or act on them. Coming and going, fear had me in bondage—in bondage and held captive in the unproductive, stagnated place called Here.

Sleeping Beauty

Fear is deadly because it has a way of lulling you to sleep, spiritually and emotionally. Thus, you check out and sleepwalk through life. I call it the "Sleeping Beauty syndrome." If you are a victim of this syndrome, you know that your life is filled with such beauty and you have beauty inside of you, but you are sleep. You are physically awake, but asleep in your emotions, your consciousness, and your purpose—asleep in life.

Fear will cause you to sleep your life away. You will consciously close your eyes to life and then open them in the place called Here. Instead of dealing with life, we let life deal with us, and we continue to sleep and stay in this place called Here. Many people hide from their problems in a spiritual and emotional sleep state. You cannot allow fear to prevent you from facing the thing or things that caused you to sleep and fail to see the beauty of living life.

Scripture speaks of the sluggard who is asleep and attached to his bed.[1] A sluggard is a person who is habitually inactive, an idler. A question is asked of the sluggard: "How long will you sleep?" That is, how long will you continue to waste away in a barren, unproductive state? Don't get me wrong, rest is good and necessary. Rest strengthens and provides a time for rejuvenation. How many times have we heard someone say or have said ourselves, "Let me rest my mind" or "Let me rest my body"? I believe that the sluggard is a metaphor for a person who has shut himself or herself off from reality and who refuses to be conscious and aware of the realities of life. Metaphorically, this person refuses to remove the denial blinders of fear and to face the ups and downs

---

[1] Proverbs 26:14.

and the good and bad feelings of life. The sluggard's sleep is stagnated and unproductive. It is a slow death of dreams, vision, and purpose.

If you have had the opportunity to view a stagnant lake, you will observe that there is no life there. Life is movement and action. Life is flowing. There is no worse feeling than to sense the beauty of purpose inside of you fighting to flow out and do what it was designed to do while you are spiritually and emotionally asleep and you either do not know how to wake up or are too fearful of waking up and truly experiencing life.

I am reminded of Langston Hughes's poem "Dream Deferred." In it, Hughes compares a deferred dream to a dried raisin, a festering sore, and rotten meat. The same is true for the beauty inside of you, if it remains stagnant.

I have experienced times in my life when I allowed fear to immobilize me: Fear of rejection, because rejection keeps you in the comfort zone afraid to step out and live. And Fear of failure, because I was so fearful of failing that I sometimes did not even try to make the simplest of moves toward my purpose.

"Worthy" Is Just a Word

Fear will distort your perception of your worthiness. Fear causes you to question whether you are worthy of love, worthy of joy, and worthy of God's blessings. Thus, you remain in the place called Here because of the lie that fear shouts: "I am a place of safety."

A feeling of unworthiness becomes the excuse for you to be average and not step out. It allows you to compromise your purpose and to doubt God's love for you.

In 2015, God spoke a life-altering word to me. Finding myself single, I began on a journey of self-discovery and self-awareness. The mask that I was wearing became too heavy. During the journey, I would spend time alone with God. In my times alone, I clearly heard His voice. So many words were spoken during those times. In my life-altering moment, God spoke,

> *You are around here praying for everybody and about everything. You believe what you pray, and you believe in Me. When you pray, you believe that I will and can do everything that you prayed about. But you only believe it for them and not for yourself. You don't truly believe that I see and love you. You don't truly believe that I will do it for you. You don't believe because you don't feel worthy.*

Every time that I reflect on what God spoke, it brings tears to my eyes. When you feel that you are not worthy, you will not ask in faith for God to do something special for you. You may ask, but you waver in your expectation of receiving what you ask for. The feeling of unworthiness overshadows your faith, and thus, you are almost afraid to ask.

Unworthiness will make you feel like you are bothering God. God is constantly telling us to come to Him, to seek Him, to knock. He says that you will find Him, that the door for whatever you need will be opened. Unworthiness stops us from falling into the arms of our Father, who not only loves, but is love.

Unworthiness tells you that God is too big, too busy, and too great for your concerns. Furthermore, you think, "Other people have needs that are more important, and I will put them ahead of mine." Who made you God? Who cast you in the role of fake martyr, where you are creating a false-humility and superiority complex because "I thought about others and sacrifice myself"? Again, I ask, who made you God? God is not a limited God. He has more than enough wisdom, time, provision, and love for every single person.

Unworthiness becomes your comfort zone that will become your prison, and eventually your grave, if you never exit the place called Here. You remain, never experiencing a full and abundant life.

We can claim several reasons and excuses, such as fear or unworthiness, for remaining in this place called Here—a stagnant place of slowly dying dreams. Some reasons may even be valid, but you owe it to yourself to wake up, come out of your state of denial and idleness, and fight like hell for the life that was prepared for you before you took your first breath.

CHAPTER 3
GET UP OR SHUT UP!

The command to get up is powerful on so many levels. It is a command to rise. When we rise, we move from a low position to a higher one. We emerge. We become stronger. Living a full life is possible when we arise in every area of our lives. When we arise in our consciousness, we are fully awake to who we are and why we are. We must arise out of difficult situations, whether they are created by others or self-imposed, that limit us and keep us small. We must arise and get up out of situations that prevent us from showing up in this life. Whether our burden is a financial issue; self-esteem issue; health issue; or a constricting, unproductive-relationship issue, we must arise.

The time to get up is now. The first step to getting up is believing that you can. Your degree of belief will determine the intensity of the fight that is needed to overcome. There is power in belief, because it provides the fuel that is needed for the fight.

You must reach a point of being sick and tired of being sick and tired, of being stuck in the foreign and unproductive place called Here. Once you believe, the next step is to follow Christ's command to the paralytic man, "Take up your pallet and walk![2] Get up!

Getting up will not be easy. Getting up will require every ounce of strength that you can muster up, and then more. Many days, I did not want to leave my bed because I did not want to face the challenges that were waiting to ambush me. On those days, remembering why I must get up was very important. To handle the outer, we must look inner. I often had to remind myself of the hidden and divine treasure that God placed in my temple. I had to remind myself that it was deposited for a purpose. Many are the afflictions and challenges that we face; however, we are called to do a great work and make the deposit on this earth that God has placed inside of us.

---

[2] John 5:8

Remember that each of us has a deposit, a treasure, on the inside of us that no one else possesses. Each of us has a purpose deposit that this earth needs. The deposit is unique and was God-prepared long before you were in the womb of your mother, long before your father met your mother, and long before your parents were in the womb.

What is your primary motivation to get up? Please do not tell me that it is to please your parents or to show an old boyfriend how you moved on. Let it be for *you*. Let it be because you are sick and tired of being sick and tired, of being average when you know that you are called to greatness. Let it be because you are sick and tired of being sick and tired of doubt and lack when you have been told that your heavenly Father owns all the cattle on a thousand hills. Let it be because you have realized that if you fail to make the deposit of the treasure that God placed inside of you, this earth will be robbed of a unique treasure. This earth will be robbed of ever feeling the essence of beauty that is you.

Rising now becomes more than just a choice; it becomes an obligation. I cannot imagine how my life would be if those who assisted me in taking off layers of pain, rejection, and low self-worth did not rise and walk in their purpose. I do not want to imagine the lives that would be affected if I had failed to arise.

Getting up requires you not to just talk about it; you must also *be* about it. You must be strategic in this battle because you are battling on several fronts. Satan, self (the ego), and society will be your biggest opponents. All three are formidable foes who do not want to let go of the old—foes who do not want to see you get up and live, but want you to stay unproductive, unsatisfied, unfulfilled, and never reaching the apex of your life.

When you realize that you have greatness inside of you—when you realize that what's on the inside of you is greater and bigger than anything that Satan, self (the ego), or society can throw at you to break you—then you will know that you are a precious jewel, a diamond. Remember, real diamonds do not break.

Fateful moments require decisions. Decide whether you will get up or shut up. Be careful how you respond because so many lives will be impacted by the choice. In the book of Genesis, Joshua told the children of Israel to "choose this day who you will serve."[3] We must choose who we will serve: will we serve the life-giver or the life-stealer? The choice must be active, vigorous, and intentional. Inactivity and doing nothing will have the same effect as choosing to spiritually and emotionally shut up and shut down.

If you choose not to get up, then physically shut up. Stop complaining about how bad and unfair things are. Stop brooding and repeating how unfair life is and how people have treated you. Stop giving other people your power, and stop blaming them for your present unpleasant state. Yes, all of it may be true: yes, maybe you were treated unfairly and should have been loved and better cared for. However, if you

---

[3] Joshua 24:15

choose not to rise out of the pain and hurt that these situations inflicted upon you, then shut up.

    Spoken words have power. Therefore, we must be mindful of the words that we speak into the atmosphere. The thing that you give the most attention will grow. As a result, the hole that you are fighting to get out of will get deeper and deeper. Our heavenly Father tells us that life and prosperity, death and destruction, have been set before us.[4] His wish is that we choose life. Choose life by choosing to get up and live.

    The tragedy is that remaining silent and shutting up prevents you from showing up in this life. You never get up. Your voice will never be heard. Your true essence will never be felt by this world. Shutting up will cause you to take to the grave the very thing, the very treasure that you were birth on this earth to leave. There are people anxiously waiting to hear your voice. I believe that when we speak and show up in purpose, we are allowing God to reveal Himself through us. God's kingdom comes, and His

---

[4] Deuteronomy 30:15.

will is done through us. Refusing to get up and remaining silent prevent God's spirit from flowing freely.

Now, I charge you to get up and live. Now, in this moment, get up. It does not matter where you are on your journey or even the challenges before you—you've got to move. Get up. Arise. Move from that low position. Become strong. Emerge. So much is resting on you rising. It is not just about you, and it never was. Arising means that you understand that you are a part of a glorious plan that is forever unfolding and revealing the awesomeness of God. Everything inside you is screaming, "Will you take your position?" "Will you fulfill your part and appear?" and "Will you arise?" All of creation groans until you arise.

For several days before God spoke the life-transforming message to me in 2015, I existed in a numbed state, going through the motions with a smiling mask that hid the deep sorrow that penetrated to my core. In the previous chapter a pivotal question was asked, "Why did I stay *Here*? I stayed in this place because I did not believe that I could leave. Because I did not believe, I did not fight for my freedom.

This was the hardest fight of my life, but I had to get up. The fight was hard because my decision to not just get up but live my life to the fullest required an emotional, physical, and spiritual shift. Because I have shifted to the "…and live" side of my life, I now know how it feels to wake up each morning with a smile on my face and excited about living this amazing gift called life.

In the pain, brokenness, disappointments, setbacks, and everything that tried to break you, get up and live. Draw on the strength of the Maker, who tells you to look to Him for your help. Scream, cry, kick, but get up and live. Once you find the strength to move forward, you'll discover that your life has changed in unimaginable ways. The next part of this book details what that new life will be like.

PART II
...AND LIVE

To live is the rarest thing in the world. Most people just exist.
—Oscar Wilde

Live life to the fullest because it only happens once.
—Unknown

When I stand before God at the end of my life, I would hope that I would not have a single bit of talent left and could say, I used everything you gave me.

—Erma Bombeck

CHAPTER 4

...WITHOUT PARALYZING FEAR

As previously stated, I found myself in a vicious cycle. My fear of failure stopped me from executing my ideas, and because I did not execute these, I failed. Thank God for power that breaks the cycle of fear.

Fear is a dream killer with a mission to convince you to remain in a low place when you feel with every fiber of your being that you were created for mountaintop living. You will never truly walk in your freedom until you conquer your fears. Life is meant to be enjoyed and lived. Fear blinds you to the possibility of achieving greatness in your life. Fear stops you from taking the first step, keeping you paralyzed in your comfort zone.

Freedom is living your dreams. Most of us are not living our God-given dreams because we are too busy living our fears; we are in the land of "what if" and "I'll never." I achieved my own freedom when I realized that I had been spiritually and emotionally paralyzed by fear; I had failed to realize that I had the keys to my chains of bondage all along—the keys of faith, courage, and love.

Key of Faith

Faith is a powerful antidote to fear. Faith removes the shackles of paralyzing fear. Once faith steps on the scene, fear runs away like a coward. Faith liberates the human spirit. Once fear is removed, there is no limit to what you can achieved. Faith says you may not know the outcome, but you are connected to someone who does. Faith says you may not feel strong enough, but you have something that is greater and stronger on the inside of you that is waiting to rise. Faith encourages, it assures, it covers, and it provides illumination to dark paths.

We must remember that fear is a valid emotion that we will feel throughout our lives. Realizing that it is a part of life, we must stand boldly and decide the role that fear will play in our lives. Will we allow fear to motivate and catapult our lives toward our destinies, or will be allow fear to paralyze us and keep up in a low place? Walking in fear is like walking in a foreign land, because we are beings created to reign in love and power, and with a sound mind. Anything contrary to this ideal is foreign.

I once read a quote that said, "Fear has two meanings: Forget everything and run, or face everything and rise." The choice is yours. Getting to your "…and live" moment requires you to rise out of fear and walk in freedom. On my journey from existing to living, I spent an enormous amount of time regretting the life-changing moments that I had failed to take advantage of and the doors that I had not walked through because of fear. I was afraid for so many reasons and on so many levels.

I embrace the fact that I am living in the "…and live" season of my life. This season is never-ending. This season only transcends higher with a final breath.

Key of Courage

Courage is a powerful key. Faith helps us to take the first step, and courage helps us take the second, third, fourth, and so on. In the face of fear, you must settle in your mind that you are going to go into your destiny anyway, trembling and all. Ambrose Redmoon spoke a quote whose words are eternal: "Courage is not the absence of fear, but rather the judgement that something else is more important than fear." Even though we all experience fear, we should not allow it to paralyze us or shrink the influence and the impact that our lives will have in the world. Courage is pulsating through our veins.

The story of Lot is an example of a life that failed to expand because of a lack of courage.[5] Not only did Lot's life shrink, but the lives of his descendants shrank too because of the lack of courage to fight paralyzing fear.

---

[5] Genesis 19:18

When I read about Lot and his predicament in Sodom and Gomorrah, I often wondered why Lot requested permission to go to Zoar, a low place. Clearly, the angels were instructed to take him to the mountain which represents higher ground. I believe that it was fear of the unknown that made Lot settle for less than what was already prepared for him and his family. Thus, Lot's entire legacy was changed. Likewise, every day we allow fear to alter our legacies, and we end up in low places as a result. When we get up and live without paralyzing fear, mountaintop living will be the norm. Zoar-level living should be the only option. Kingdom living is an expectation. Utilize your key to access the higher ground that you were destined to occupy.

As Anais Nin said, "Life shrinks or expands in proportion to one's courage."

Key of Love

Love is the greatest key. Love covers a multitude of sins, and it opens every heart door. Love is a universal key available to every human being who dares to possess it. In my lifetime, I have witnessed love stand strong in the face of fear many times. It is love that fuels the drive to keep trying, to never give up, and to get back up after falling an unmeasurable amount of times.

We are told to love our neighbors like we love ourselves. How do we love our neighbor and see the value of our neighbor if we don't know how to love ourselves or see our own value every time we look in the mirror?

The "…and live" side of your life requires that you love yourself—that you love yourself enough to keep getting up each morning with such zeal to fulfill your purpose, even in the face of uncertainty; that you love yourself enough to keep getting up when life knocks you down again and again. Loves reveals the beauty. When you see your beauty, the beauty in others will also be revealed. Love makes life worth living. An "…and live" mentality about life changes the lens in which we view life and people. It allows us to view life through the lens of love.

Love is the greatest key because everything in life hinges on love. The sun rises and sets because of love. We are here on the earth because of love. Every breath that we take is because of love. When we close our eyes in this existence, they will close in love and open beholding the greatest love of all.

Understanding the awesomeness of the Creator and grasping the truth that in His awesomeness He truly loves us is liberating. He is not only able to love you, but He is more than able to show you why He loves. Knowing that you are loved in a majestic way gives you the power to face fear head-on. In reminding ourselves of who we are, we are reminded that we were not given a spirit of paralyzing fear, but love along with courageous power and a sound mind of faith.

CHAPTER 5

...WITHOUT PAIN

The pain from life's disappointments and challenges comes from spiritual and emotional wounds. Nevertheless, wounds can heal. When you decide to get up and live the life that you were meant to live, the deep wounds begin to heal. For much of my life, I believed that pain was life. I remember being in so much pain it was hard to breathe. I held my breath, physically and spiritually, hoping that holding my breath was the solution to stopping the pain. I allowed pain to silence my voice.

Crossing over into "…and live" territory will change your perspective on pain. Now I understand that pain is a part of life. Life can be beautiful once you understand that pain has a purpose: Pain can be a propeller. Pain can propel you into your destiny, into your purpose. Pain can be the motivator that causes you to pull away from the pitfalls of life. Just as pain silenced me, by embracing and allowing pain to flow in its purpose, I exhaled. I exhaled the sadness, doubts, and feelings of unworthiness that once resided deep within me. Embracing the pain helped me discover my true voice, the voice that speaks from my heart.

A spiritual and emotional wound hurts just as much as a physical wound. Although the method of healing varies, healing is inevitable. Often, scars are proof that healing has begun. Just like I have physical scars from falls and mishaps I have experienced throughout my life, I have emotional scars as well. Scars are a part of the journey of living. I am thankful for the gifts of healing and wholeness. My scars are beautiful because they remind me that I made it. They remind me that I am healed. They remind me that I am strong. My scars remind me that I am alive. As I walk through this life, I will not hide my scars, because they are beautiful. Each scar has a unique story and lesson. My scars' beauty lies in every growth, increase, enlargement, and breakthrough that I have experienced. Although invisible to the human eyes, my scars are seen with the heart. My beautiful scars allow me to show my victories and my breakthroughs with the hope of helping someone else get up and live. My scars are proof that you can get up, and not only just get up, but live a victorious life.

Tears are also a part of the journey. It has been said that tears wash the soul. One of the beautiful missions of tears is to release and wash away pain. On this journey, I have shed so many tears: tears for pain experienced in broken relationships, disappointing situations, unexpected losses, and much more—whether this pain was at the forefront or it had to be uncovered. When you decide to get up and live, you must get up out of the pain. Getting up requires you to face the pain. The pain that you allowed to take up residence in your heart must be evicted. Let pain flow through you and fuel your purpose. Every tear that was shed was necessary and had a purpose. I will never know the individual purpose of each tear, but God sees and knows the purpose of each one of them. He knows, and I want to believe that He catches each one.

As painful memories and bruises are revealed, feel the pain and let them flow through you. There will be times when you feel like shedding tears. Let them flow as well. Tears remind that you are no longer numb, but you feel and you are alive. Never mind how it looks to other people; that is not your concern. I am amazed at the number of family and friends who have shared with me that it has been years since they have cried. So many others cry in silence; I was one of them.

From my childhood, I believed that crying was a sign of weakness. I remember going to funerals and biting my tongue to keep from crying. How many of us go through life, painful situation after painful situation, while biting our tongues and allowing pain to fester inside.

Arising and taking control of your life is freedom. Freedom means no more tongue biting, no more hiding, no more hopeless crying. Freedom is life. We all shed tears; however, we are told not to weep like we have no hope. You have everything that you need inside of you to get up and live the beautiful life that God destined for you to live. And crippling pain is not in the plan.

CHAPTER 6

...IN PEACE

Living in peace is not living in denial that unpleasant situations are happening around us. Living with peace means living with the assurance that a higher power is at work and is causing all things to work in our favor. It is acknowledging that you know your lane and that traveling in someone else's lane is unwise, because you are not equipped for the unique purpose of that lane. Surely, traveling in God's lane is not an option. You are not all-seeing, all-knowing, or all-powerful. Living with peace means you know your lane, and you walk in your lane only, with all the setbacks and victories that this life presents.

Peace is assurance. When you have assurance, you are not so much concerned about the how and the when because you know who is responsible for the how and the when. You know that the one who is responsible is faithful. We have the assurance that every promise that the Father made to us is "yes" and "amen." Living with peace means being confident that you are enough. In your core, at the center of your being, you are enough. Enough means not too much and not too little. In all your unique, quirky ways, you are enough. Being enough gives you a feeling of assurance. Being enough means being satisfied.

Peace is the ability to trust. Learning trust is the first step toward living in peace. Understanding trust is knowing who and what to trust. Trust is having a firm belief in the reliability, truth, ability, or strength of someone or something. Trust in the reliability of God is peace. Trust in the ability and strength of God is peace. Knowing that God is truth is beyond peace. Total trust in God is surrendering your heart, mind, and soul.

Surrendering control was not easy for me. I believed that if I relinquished control, I would be vulnerable, and being vulnerable was a sign of weakness. One of the many lessons that I learned was that surrender is a power position. It is a position of peace. My life has been a string of inconsistencies. Because my choices, my family life, friendships, career, and romances have been inconsistent and unreliable, my ability to trust was damaged. I was always questioning people's motives and acts of kindness. My peace came when I understood God's love and faithfulness. I am assured that I could never go wrong with putting my trust in a God who truly loves me long before I took my first breath, a God who has never failed me, a Father who has seen my vulnerabilities and weaknesses countless times and who still loves me. Now that is peace!

Peace is loving yourself. I mentioned earlier that I lived life questioning the motives of others and their acts of kindness. I was paranoid and unable to receive the simplest of things, such as a compliment, an unexpected gift, or love. Loving yourself helps you understand that you are worthy. It helps you understand that you are beautiful and unique. Loving yourself means loving all of you, the good and the bad, the self that makes you smile and the self that makes you weep. When you love yourself, you will then be able to love others and see the beauty and treasure in their lives.

Peace comes because you understand that you no longer live life on guard, as if everyone is out to get you. There is a special kind of peace when you know yourself, know why you are living and breathing, and know that the treasure that you have inside is unique and necessary. Yes, there will be moments when your intuition is correct regarding certain people with bad motives and intentions. However, there is still peace even with that revelation because loving yourself gives you the ability to love all people. Love up close and love from afar, but love.

Living with peace gives you a greater understanding of the psalmist's phrase that speaks of peace flowing like a river: calm and gentle, yet free and adventurously forging through new territory; meandering and continuously flowing to something greater. Living with peace is allowing this river to flow through you into the lives of others and into the world. Peace could not flow if I did not first get up. I did. I got up, and now I live with peace. Living with peace gives you a greater appreciation of the promise of peace that surpasses all understanding, that perfect, ultimate peace.

CHAPTER 7
...LIKE IT'S GOLDEN

A golden life is a happy and successful life: a life not measured by physical possessions but by joy and wholeness; a shimmering life that shines for all to see; but most of all, a life that fulfills its purpose and glorifies God. Real gold shimmers and has value. You must value every moment of your life. Your input has value. Your ideas have value. Your purpose has value. Your deposit that you make on this earth has value. Your worth was predetermined. You are the one that will determine what version of you that this world will get. Never let anyone or anything dull your shine.

For so many years, I hid the golden light that my Father destined to shine and shimmer through me. I was aimlessly and unproductively standing in the dark, unable to be the illuminating light that I was created to be.

Throughout history, people have associated gold, or being golden, with being good: we speak of a golden sun, golden voice, golden generation, or golden opportunity. My favorite is the golden age or era. My own golden age was a time of great happiness, peace, prosperity, creativity, and major achievements. I reached a point in my journey that I asked myself, "Why do my times of peace, happiness, prosperity, and achievements have to be limited? Why can't it be a constant flow, a golden lifestyle?"

    Living life like it's golden requires us to seize every moment of life, every moment and every opportunity to create satisfying and joyful memories that bring smiles to our faces. These memory moments make you laugh when you feel like crying, make you carry on when you feel like throwing in the towel. On this journey, there have been many things that I discovered about myself: I realized that I was living a hurried life. I realized that I did not stop to smell the beautiful flowers that God placed in my life; I was not even aware they were there. (Flowers are people and situations that are strategically placed and orchestrated in your life to awaken and resuscitate you.) In previous times, tears would well up in my eyes when I thought about the opportunities for love and for deeper relationships and other destiny-changing moments that I did not seize in my life. Refusing to get up will keep you wondering how your life could have been, and you will forever live in the regretful past. Living will help you move from the land of regret and seize the moment of a hopeful future. Make it golden—live in the now and experience moments in your life that take your breath away.

And live. Living like it's golden means seizing every moment of life. Cherish every breath, every heartbeat. Find joy in the simple and small things in life. I find joy in feeling the wind against my cheeks. I find joy in hearing laughter. I find joy in hearing my grandmother, who has lived on this earth for ninety-one years, tell me that she loves me. I find joy in the free, courageous woman I have become. I even find joy in my pain, because now I know that it has a purpose, like everything God has created. So, now I allow it to flow through me and not take up residence. I allow pain to be a teacher. I find joy in every breath I take. My breaths are not promised, but they let me know that I am still here and that there is still purpose in me. My breaths remind me that I am more than a conqueror. Most of all, I am overjoyed that I can shine, shimmer, and be me. That is living life like it's golden, shining in my truth for the entire world to see—not for my own glory, but in the light of God's glory.

Embrace the person you are in this moment. Embrace the person you are becoming. Embrace the free and unhindered person who you are presenting to the world. Stand in your truth, and give to the world nothing less than your best. Shine and be bold. Never ask anyone's permission to be you; just *be*. Never ask anyone's permission to shine. Just shine—and be great!

FINAL THOUGHT

The journey of living life begins with an awakening. My prayer is that this book is instrumental in your awakening process. The journey can be uncomfortable at times, but stay the course, because it is also beautiful. Keep your eyes on the prize, on the finished course of a fulfilled and purpose-accomplished life. It is time to exhale; you no longer need to hold your breath in, waiting to live your best life. To everything there is a season, an appointed time. This is your appointed time to live.

Finally, I present to you my wish list:

- I wish that you would stop and not only view the roses that have been strategically placed on your journey but that you also smell, touch, and experience the warmth of each rose.

- I wish that the eyes of your enlightenment be opened and that revelations will flow freely.

- I wish that you remember and grow from every lesson learned on your journey.

- I wish that you savor the sweet memories obtained on this journey so that, on days of contradiction, they will put a smile on your face.

- I wish that every spiritual birth that you experience brings you joy and expands you.
- I wish that your days of contradiction work in your favor and for your good.
- I wish that every hindrance that has stopped you in the past be removed.
- I wish that you meet the person, inside of you, who you were always meant to be.
- I wish that you experience beautiful moments in your life that take your breath away.
- I wish that you would always dance in the rainstorms of life.
- I wish you peace that surpasses all understanding.
- I wish you wholeness.
- I wish that you prosper in all your ways.
- I wish you *love*.

You have been given everything that you need so that you might live and walk in dominion. God has already provided you with everything that you need to walk in your purpose and make your unique deposit in this earth. Every provision that you need for your vision, whether spiritual or physical, was granted from the foundations of the earth. No more excuses; now go shine. Get up and live. Live victoriously. Live fearlessly. Live unapologetically. Most importantly, *live*!

www.ingramcontent.com/pod-product-compliance
Lightning Source LLC
LaVergne TN
LVHW020101090426
835510LV00040B/2766